Collins

Cherry Blossoms

English Workbook

LKG

FS2

SERIES EDITOR: RANI THIPPAVAZZULA

Note to Facilitator

Dear Facilitator,

Here are a few activities that you can conveniently do with your child. These activities can be done using the flash cards and simple materials available at home. These activities are designed to cater to the development of a variety of skills that go beyond literacy and numeracy. You can do these activities in any order. Depending on the interest of the child, you could repeat the activities. You could also tweak them to make them more enjoyable.

1. **Show and tell:** Hold up the letter flashcards, one at a time. Say the letter name and sound aloud. Ask your child to repeat after you. Encourage your child to trace the letter with their index finger. Point to the objects whose names start with the same letter.
2. **Matching letters to their sounds:** Place a few flashcards on a flat surface. Say the sound of a letter. Ask the child to pick up the correct flashcard. You could alternate between the letter names and the letter sounds.
3. **Arranging flashcards:** Jumble up all the letter flashcards. Ask your child to arrange them in the correct sequence.
4. **Guess the letter:** Lay the flashcards face down on a surface. Ask the children to look at the picture and guess the letter. Then ask them to point at the correct letter.
5. **Listen and say:** Close your eyes or tie a blindfold over your eyes. Ask the child to pick up a flashcard. Ask them to describe the picture. Guess the letter displayed on the flashcard by listening to the description. You can take turns with your child to play this game.
6. **Letters/Sounds in nature:** Take children for a walk outside. Ask them to name the different things they see. As they become familiar, ask them to match the initial sound in the names to the correct letter flashcard. For example, 'leaf' should be matched to the flashcard for the letter l.
7. **Treasure hunt:** Make a simple sand pit using a tray and hide the letter flash cards inside it. Call out a letter and let your child find that letter card from the sand pit.
8. **Finger printing letters:** Give your child a piece of paper with all the letters written/printed on it, water/poster colours. Show a letter flashcard and guide the child to fingerprint the corresponding letter (with only forefinger). Use this activity to familiarise the child with capital and small letters.

9. **Naming pictures and matching letters:** Cut out pictures of familiar objects from old magazines, newspapers, etc. Ask the child to name the object in the picture and place the corresponding letter flashcard next to it. Should you desire, you could also do this using real objects present in the room.

Getting Ready to Write Letters

10. **Trace sand paper letters:** You can make sand paper cut-outs of letters. Ask your child to trace the letters on the flashcards. Then ask them to trace the sand paper letters using the same motion. Repeat this frequently. This will enable your child to become familiar with the formation of letters.

11. **Sensory activity with tracing letters on sand-tray:** Give your child letter flashcards and a sand-tray/plate filled with beans to see and trace letters. Once they can do this, you can give them big chalks and ask them to write on slates or write on mud using sticks. The children can use the flashcards for reference.

12. **Playdough letters:** Provide your child with playdough. Show your child a letter flashcard. Ask them to make the letter using playdough and point to an object whose name starts with the letter.

13. **Crayon colouring:** Place a box of crayons along with a few scraps of paper on a table. Encourage your child to scribble, doodle, and/or draw anything they like. Focus on whether they are holding the pencil correctly between their thumb, index finger and middle finger.

14. **Writing activity with slate and chalk:** Give your child a slate and a few differently coloured chalk sticks. Give them a letter card for reference. Ask them to write the letter on the slate with your guidance. This writing-readiness activity will help children in developing the fine motor skills required to hold a pencil and write.

Getting Ready to Read Words (For older children)

15. **Chunking sounds:** Place a letter flashcard (a consonant) on a table. Ask your child to say the letter sound. Place another letter card (a vowel). Demonstrate how to chunk the two sounds together. Allow the child to change the letters randomly and read aloud. Gradually, add the third letter so that the child can read a complete word independently. Use the cards with letter combinations for longer words. (Allow the child to read the word formed, even if it is not a word. This activity is designed to enable children to read independently.)

16. **Building sentences:** Use a combination of picture and letter cards to encourage your child to build sentences independently. Once the child is familiar with this activity, stress on the need to add a full stop at the end of a sentence or a question mark at the end of a question.

Contents

LETTERS A, B, C, D, E, F

Draw a picture starting with the following letters.

A

ant

B

butterfly

Trace and write the letters.

C

D

E

F

LETTERS G, H, I, J, K, L

Trace and write the letters.

G 

H 

I 

J 

K 

L 

LETTERS M, N, O, P, Q, R

Write the beginning letter of the following pictures.

N O P Q R S T U V W X Y Z

LETTERS S, T, U, V

Draw pictures with the given letters.

S

T

U

V

LETTERS W, X, Y, Z

Read the letters.

W  watch

X  x-mas tree

Y  yo-yo

Z  zebra

Ring the odd one out.

W   

X 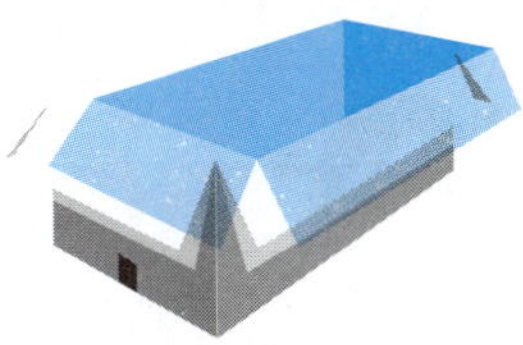  

Y 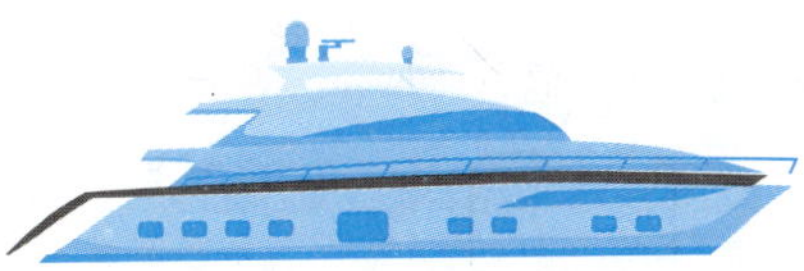  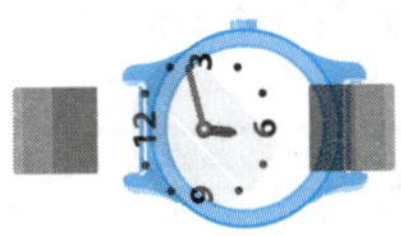

PRONOUNS

Read the pronouns.

I you he

she we you

they

Match the following.

he • 

she • 

we • 

Tick (✓) the correct option.

I am a

 ☐

 ☐

ACTION WORDS

Match the words to the correct activities.

swim •	• 
sit •	• 
dance •	• 
sleep •	• 
run •	• 

POSITION WORDS

Read these words. Match the words to the pictures.

behind | under | inside | front | beside | on | between

Draw a ball under the table.

NEAR AND FAR

Match the following.

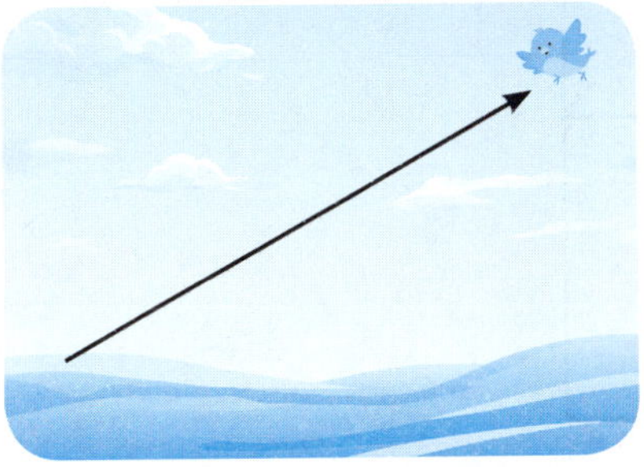

far

near

HELLO LETTERS a and b

Trace and write.

a	a	a	a	a
a	a	a	a	a

Trace and write.

b	b	b	b	b
b	b	b	b	b

HELLO LETTERS c and d

Trace and write.

c	c	c	c	c
c	c	c	c	c

Trace and write.

d	d	d	d	d
d	d	d	d	d

HELLO LETTERS e and f

Trace and write.

e	e	e	e	e
e	e	e	e	e

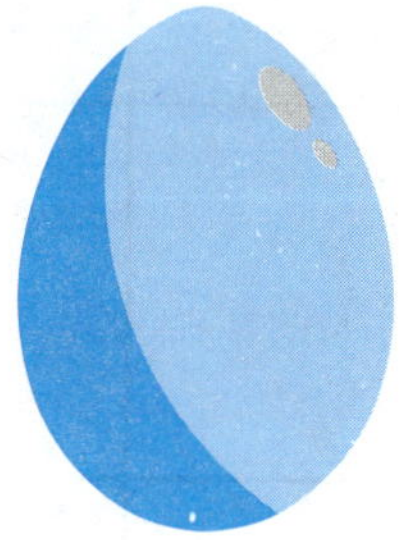

Trace and write.

f	f	f	f	f
f	f	f	f	f

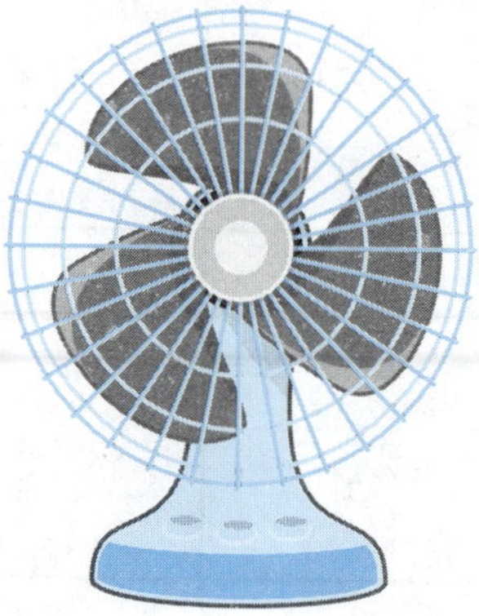

HELLO LETTERS g and h

Trace and write.

g	g	g	g	g
g	g	g	g	g

Trace and write.

h	h	h	h	h
h	h	h	h	h

HELLO LETTERS i and j

Trace and write.

i	i	i	i	i
i	i	i	i	i

Trace and write.

j	j	j	j	j
j	j	j	j	j

HELLO LETTERS k and l

Trace and write.

k	k	k	k	k
k	k	k	k	k

Trace and write.

l	l	l	l	l
l	l	l	l	l

HELLO LETTERS m and n

Trace and write.

m	m	m	m	m
m	m	m	m	m

Trace and write.

n	n	n	n	n
n	n	n	n	n

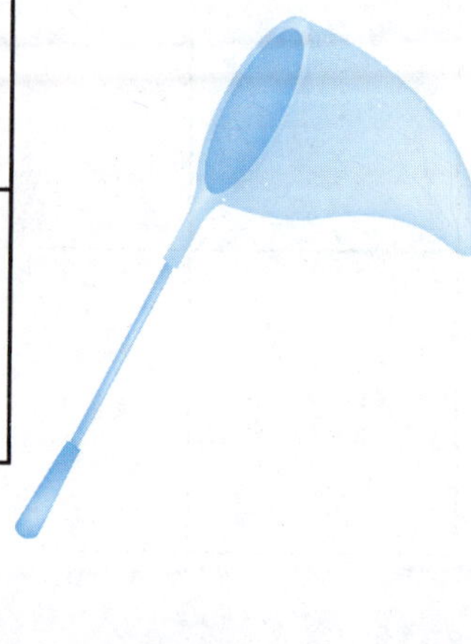

HELLO LETTERS o and p

Trace and write.

o	o	o	o	o
o	o	o	o	o

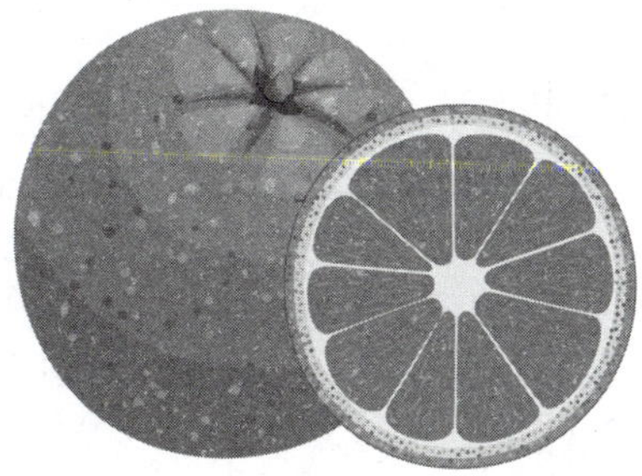

Trace and write.

p	p	p	p	p
p	p	p	p	p

HELLO LETTERS q and r

Trace and write.

q	q	q	q	q
q	q	q	q	q

Trace and write.

r	r	r	r	r
r	r	r	r	r

HELLO LETTERS s and t

Trace and write.

s	s	s	s	s
s	s	s	s	s

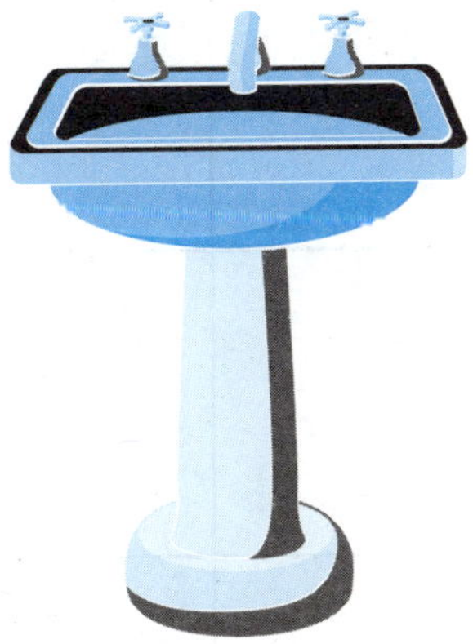

Trace and write.

t	t	t	t	t
t	t	t	t	t

HELLO LETTERS u and v

Trace and write.

u	u	u	u	u
u	u	u	u	u

Trace and write.

v	v	v	v	v
v	v	v	v	v

HELLO LETTERS w and x

Trace and write.

w	w	w	w	w
w	w	w	w	w

Trace and write.

x	x	x	x	x
x	x	x	x	x

HELLO LETTERS y and z

Trace and write.

y	y	y	y	y
y	y	y	y	y

Trace and write.

z	z	z	z	z
z	z	z	z	z

CVC WORDS WITH 'a'

Match the words to the pictures.

- pan
- dad
- cap
- fan
- cat
- mat

Complete the word.

☐ a ☐

☐ a ☐

☐ a ☐

☐ a ☐

CVC WORDS WITH 'e'

Read the words. Match the rhyming words.

peg	leg
fed	red
bet	net
hen	den

Complete the word.

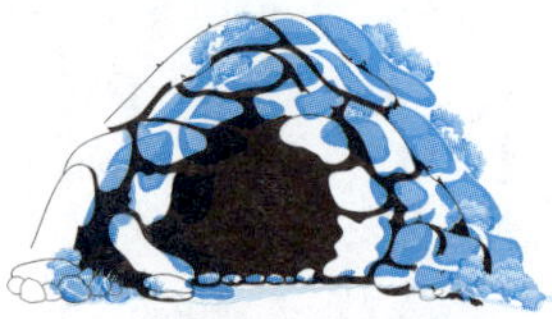

☐ e ☐

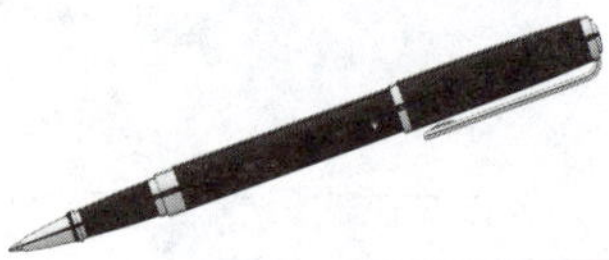

☐ e ☐

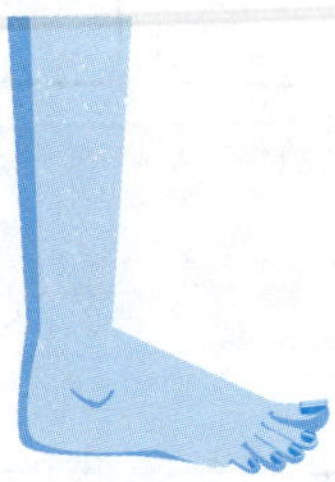

☐ e ☐

☐ e ☐

CVC WORDS WITH 'i'

Read the words.

bib	is	lip
kid	bit	fig
pin	rib	his
tip	lid	fit
big	bin	

Match the following.

 • • lid

 • • pin

 • • kid

CVC WORDS WITH 'O'

Read the words. Match the rhyming words.

sob •	• mob
hot •	• cot
pod •	• nod
dog •	• fog
hop •	• pop

Draw picture of the given words.

pot	dog
log	cot

A B C D E F G H I J K L M

CVC WORDS WITH 'u'

Read the words. Match the rhyming words.

tub	rub
jug	hug
pup	cup
bun	run
hut	nut

Fill the missing letters.

c		p

s	u	

	u	g

	u	b

	u	n

h		t

b	u	

b		d

	u	d

N O P Q R S T U V W X Y Z

I KNOW CVC WORDS

Look at the pictures. Complete the words.

 t [ ] b	 t [ ] p	 c [ ] p
 b [ ] s	 c [ ] p	 t [ ] p
 h [ ] n	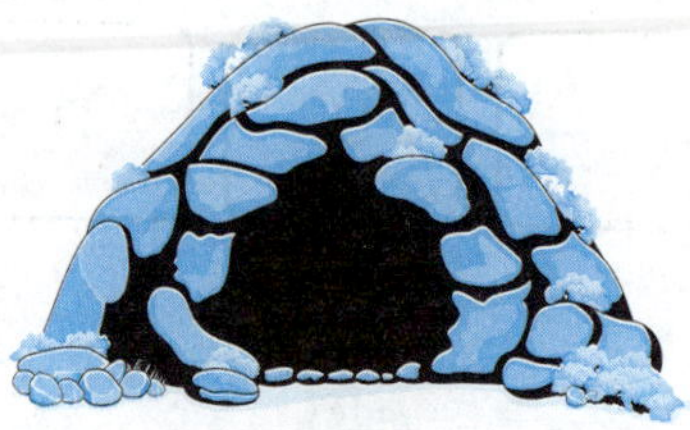 d [ ] n	 h [ ] t

A B C D E F G H I J K L M

b | | n

c | | t

t | | n

b | | n

s | | n

r | | t

p | | t

c | | t

l | | d

s | | t

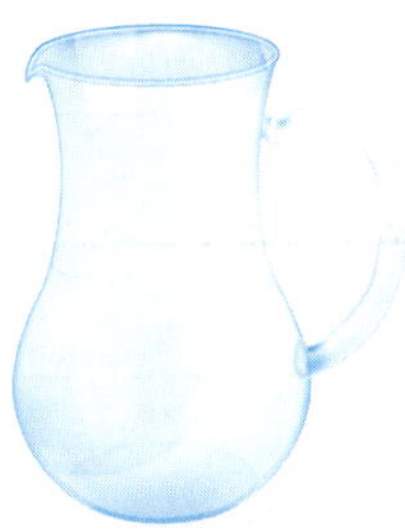

j | | g

d | | g

SIGHT WORDS

Trace and write.

boy	boy		
girl	girl		
she	she		
this	this		
that	that		

LETTERS a to z

Write the letters.

a 

b 

c 

d 

e 

f 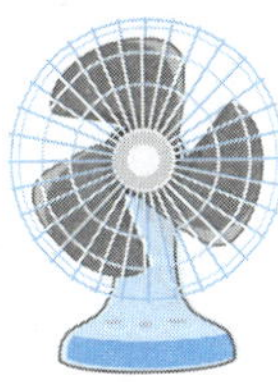

g 

h 

i 

j 

k 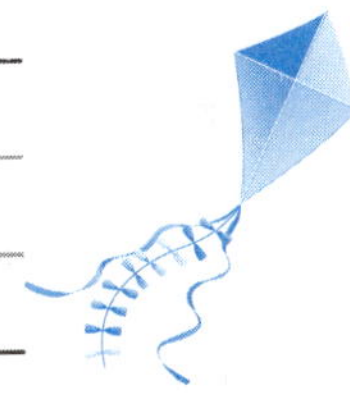

l 

m 

n 

o o

p p

q q

r r

s s

t t

u u

v v

w w

x x

y y

z z